Baptism
Helpful Answers to Common Questions

Allen Duty

Copyright Page

Baptism: Helpful Answers to Common Questions
Copyright © 2011 by New Life Baptist Church
Published by lulu.com

All rights reserved. No part of this publication may be reproduced, stored in a retrieval system, or transmitted in any form by any means, electronic, mechanical, photocopy, recording, or otherwise, without the prior permission of the publisher, except as provided for by USA copyright law.

Cover Design: Charlie Apel

First Printing: 2011

Printed in the United States of America

Unless otherwise indicated, Scripture quotations are from The Holy Bible, English Standard Version®, copyright 2001 by crossway Bibles, a publishing ministry of Good News Publishers. Used by permission. All rights reserved.

All emphases in Scripture quotations have been added by the author.

ISBN 978-1-4583-7369-4

Dedication

To my beautiful wife, Kendra, who loves the Lord Jesus and serves Him wholeheartedly. I adore you.

To my children, all unique blessings from God. You bring me great joy.

To the elders at New Life Baptist Church, my co-laborers in Christ. Your service to the local church is humbling and Christ-exalting. Thank you for all you do.

To the members at New Life Baptist Church, the flock I am privileged to serve as a pastor. I hope to serve you until Jesus calls me home.

Contents

Introduction   7

Section One: What is Baptism?

1 Baptism is an Ordinance   11

2 Baptism is a Symbol of Regeneration   15

Section Two: How Should Baptism Be Observed?

3 Whom Should Be Baptized?   23

4 How Should We Baptize?   31

5 When Should We Baptize?   35

Appendix

Answers to Specific Questions about Baptism   41

Introduction
What's the Big Deal?

If you grew up in the western hemisphere, there is a good chance that you have had some firsthand experience with baptism. Perhaps you were baptized as a believer, or attended the baptism service of someone who was. Maybe your parents had you baptized as an infant, or you were invited to attend a baptism service for a niece or nephew. Possibly you have even heard of the "Certificate of Debaptism," first produced by The National Secular Society in England a few years ago.[1]

Whatever the case, it is likely that you have had some exposure to baptism. However, it is equally likely that you have some lingering questions about baptism. What is it? Is it important? Does it matter how baptism is observed, or even if it is observed at all?

Even if you are a committed follower of Christ who has been baptized, you may have some of these same questions or others like them. This short book is an attempt to do exactly what the title suggests: to provide helpful answers to common questions about baptism. In order to do this, we will explore the Bible's teaching on the nature of baptism and on how baptism is to be observed. It is my hope that God will use this book to help you answer these basic questions as well as several specific questions you or others you know may be asking. Thanks for taking the time to read this book, and may God bless you as you seek to know and obey His will.

---

[1] *National Secular Society*, "Debaptise Yourself!," http://www.secularism.org.uk/debaptise-yourself.html. (accessed October 1, 2009).

Section One
What is Baptism?

1

Baptism is an Ordinance

All Christians, Catholic and protestant, agree that baptism was commanded by Jesus Christ and therefore is a non-negotiable element of faithful Christian practice. Some traditions, primarily those in the Roman Catholic church, refer to baptism as a "sacrament," while others, such as Southern Baptists, refer to it as an "ordinance." In using the term "sacrament," many Roman Catholic theologians mean that baptism is essential to salvation. Protestants would reject that understanding of baptism on biblical grounds, which will be clearly explained in chapter two. With respect to the terminology itself, however, I am in agreement with Wayne Grudem: "If we are willing to explain clearly what we mean, it does not seem to make any difference whether we use the word sacrament or not."[2] Since the term "sacrament" can be confusing for those familiar with Roman Catholic theology, I will refer to baptism as an "ordinance" because baptism was ordained (that is, "decreed" or "commanded") by Jesus and taught as an ordinance by the apostles and New Testament writers. We will now explore this idea by testing it against Scripture.

Jesus Taught Baptism as an Ordinance

In Matthew 28:18-20, Jesus gives what is known as the Great Commission. He states,

---

[2] Wayne Grudem, *Systematic Theology* (Grand Rapids: Zondervan, 1994), 966.

All authority in heaven and on earth has been given to me. Go therefore and make disciples of all nations, baptizing them in the name of the Father and of the Son and of the Holy Spirit, teaching them to observe all that I have commanded you. And behold, I am with you always, to the end of the age.

Jesus claimed to be and proved Himself to be God.[3] On his own authority as God, he commanded his disciples to disciple others, baptizing them in the name of the Father, Son, and Holy Spirit. He ordained baptism as the signifying mark of a believer, and as such, everyone who confesses Christ as Lord should be baptized.

The Apostles Taught Baptism as an Ordinance

Jesus was not alone in teaching baptism as an ordinance. After preaching to the crowd gathered at Pentecost, the people who believed Peter's words asked what they should do. Peter declared, "Repent and be baptized every one of you in the name of Jesus Christ for the forgiveness of your sins, and you will receive the gift of the Holy Spirit" (Acts 2:38). Peter didn't say that they could be baptized if they felt like it, or if it didn't cause too much inconvenience or stress. He stated it as a command, just as Jesus had done in Matthew 28.

Paul's experience also shows that baptism is an ordinance. After Jesus appears to him on the road to Damascus, he is blinded and led into a city where a man named Ananias comes to him. Ananias preaches the Gospel to Paul, and Luke notes, "And immediately something like scales fell from his eyes, and he regained his sight. *Then he rose and was baptized*; and taking food, he was strengthened" (Acts 9:18-19). Without delay,

---

[3] Matt. 1:23, 26:63-65; Mk 10:17-18, 14:61-64; Jn. 5:18, 6:38, 6:41-46, 14:6, 20:28, et.al.

Paul is baptized. Recounting the experience years later, Paul notes that Ananias had said to him, "And now why do you wait? Rise and be baptized and wash away your sins, calling on his name" (Acts 22:16). The apostles most certainly understood baptism to be an ordinance.

The New Testament Writers Taught Baptism as an Ordinance

In agreement with Jesus' teaching and the apostles' preaching, the writers of the New Testament affirmed baptism as an ordinance. Writing to the Colossians, Paul states,

> In him you were also circumcised with a circumcision made without hands, by putting off the body of the flesh, by the circumcision of Christ, having been buried with him in baptism, in which you were also raised with him through faith in the powerful working of God, who raised him from the dead (2:11-12).

Paul had never met these believers (cf. 1:3-8, 2:1), and yet he simply assumed that they had been baptized because the members of the early church understood baptism as an ordinance, not as a suggestion.

Further, Paul clearly teaches baptism as an ordinance in Romans 6:1-4. There he states that those who have been baptized into Christ Jesus were baptized into death. It is apparent from Paul's wording that baptism was simply expected of every believer, since it is the way that one showed that he or she had been buried with Christ in death and raised to walk in new life through faith in Christ.

Peter is equally clear that baptism is an ordinance in 1 Peter 3:18-22. In this passage, Peter states, "Baptism…now saves you, not as a removal of dirt from the body but as an appeal to God for a good conscience, through the resurrection of Jesus Christ" (v. 21). Peter is bold enough to say that baptism saves – not the act itself, but what it *represents*: an appeal to God for a good conscience. Baptism is the outward demonstration of what God has done inwardly in every believer, and as such is an ordinance for every believer.

Summary and A Look Ahead

Jesus, the apostles, and the New Testament writers taught baptism as an ordinance. All Catholic Christians and Protestant Christians agree that baptism should be observed by all believers. Since baptism is an ordinance, it should not be regarded as a suggestion or the mark of a "super-disciple" of Jesus. Rather, baptism is the joyful duty of every believer.

In the next chapter, we will examine the Scriptures to prove that baptism is not salvific (i.e. a work that earns God's saving grace) but rather symbolic of the work Christ has already done in the life of a believer.

2

Baptism is a Symbol of Regeneration

Clearly, the Scriptures set forth baptism as an ordinance. However, professing Christians disagree on the nature of baptism. Some, such as Roman Catholics and members of the Church of Christ, argue that baptism is necessary for salvation.[4] Others believe that baptism is symbolic of the work Christ has already accomplished in a believer. In order to determine which view is correct, we will examine both views in light of Scripture.

Baptism: Necessary Work or Important Symbol?

The salvific view of baptism teaches that baptism actually saves its recipients by conferring the grace of Christ. Fundamentally, proponents of this belief are saying that people are saved by faith in Christ plus works (namely participation in baptism, likely along with other works). Whether one was saved by faith alone or by faith plus works was the question at the center of the protestant reformation of the 16th century. Wayne Grudem summarizes the debate well:

> Martin Luther's great concern was to teach that salvation depends on faith alone, not on faith *plus works*. But if baptism and participating in the other sacraments are *necessary for salvation*

---

[4] See, for example, the official Church of Christ teaching at http://church-of-christ.org/church-of-christ/JMB.html. It explicitly states, "You should know that by baptism you are saved from sins, you have remission of sins, sins are washed away by the blood of Christ," etc. While individual members of the Church of Christ may believe differently, the church's official position is that baptism is necessary for salvation.

because they are *necessary* for receiving grace, then salvation really is based on faith plus works (emphasis mine).[5]

The Scriptures are abundantly clear that baptism does not confer grace to its recipients, and as such is not essential for salvation. When Jesus was crucified, he was hung between two criminals. Though both men mocked him at first (Matthew 27:44), one of the thieves repented and asked Jesus to remember him when Jesus entered his kingdom. Jesus responded, "Truly, I say to you, today you will be with me in Paradise" (Luke 23:43). This thief was *never* baptized, yet Jesus *assures* the thief he will be with him in Paradise. Additionally, Paul states in 1 Corinthians 1,

> I thank God that I baptized none of you except Crispus and Gaius, so that no one may say that you were baptized in my name. (I did baptize also the household of Stephanas. Beyond that, I do not know whether I baptized anyone else.) For Christ did not send me to baptize *but to preach the gospel...* (14-17a).

In Paul's mind, baptism is distinct from the gospel. Obviously, Paul thought it was important: he himself was baptized, he baptized others, and he taught others to baptize. However, Paul never taught that baptism was essential to salvation – in fact, he taught exactly the opposite.

Paul and the New Testament writers clearly taught that salvation was the gracious gift of God, and not earned by works of any kind. Here

---

[5] Grudem, *Systematic Theology*, 973.

are just a few examples of New Testament teaching about salvation by grace and through faith:

> What then shall we say was gained by Abraham, our forefather according to the flesh? For if Abraham was justified by works, he has something to boast about, but not before God. For what does the Scripture say? "*Abraham believed God, and it was counted to him as righteousness.*" Now to the one who works, his wages are not counted as a gift but as his due. And to the one who does not work but believes in him who justifies the ungodly, *his faith is counted as righteousness*, just as David also speaks of the blessing of the one to whom God counts righteousness apart from works: "Blessed are those whose lawless deeds are forgiven, and whose sins are covered; blessed is the man against whom the Lord will not count his sin (Romans 4:1-8).

> We ourselves are Jews by birth and not Gentile sinners; yet *we know that a person is not justified by works of the law but through faith in Jesus Christ*, so we also have believed in Christ Jesus, in order to be justified by faith in Christ and not by works of the law, because by works of the law no one will be justified (Galatians 2:15-16).

> For by grace you have been saved through faith. And this is not your own doing; it is the gift of God, *not a result of works*, so that no one may boast (Ephesians 2:8-9).

> For we ourselves were once foolish, disobedient, led astray, slaves to various passions and pleasures, passing our days in malice and envy, hated by others and hating one another. But when the goodness and loving kindness of God our Savior appeared, he saved us, *not because of works done by us in righteousness, but according to his own mercy*, by the washing of regeneration and renewal of the Holy Spirit, whom he poured out on us richly through Jesus Christ our Savior, so that being justified by his grace we might become heirs according to the hope of eternal life (Titus 3:3-7).

> Baptism, which corresponds to this [i.e. Noah's flood], now saves you, *not as a removal of dirt from the body but as an appeal to God for a good conscience*, through the resurrection of Jesus Christ (1 Peter 3:21).

It is abundantly clear from these passages that salvation is the gift of God, and that no work – including even one commanded by Christ – is necessary for salvation. Baptism is certainly a mark of obedience to which every believer should gladly submit, but it cannot and does not earn the favor of God.

Summary and A Look Ahead

There is overwhelming evidence from Scripture that a person is saved by grace alone, through faith alone, apart from any works. Baptism is an ordinance of Christ and the most important physical representation of salvation, but it is a work of faith, and as such does not earn the favor of God.

In section two, we will seek to answer the question, "How should baptism be observed?" I will give answers to the three most important questions under that larger question, namely:

1) Whom should be baptized? (Chapter 3)

2) How should we baptize? (Chapter 4)

3) When should we baptize? (Chapter 5)

While all Protestants would (or should) agree with what has been said in the first two chapters, genuine believers disagree about the answers to the questions in the next three chapters. We are persuaded of the baptistic position (which is held by far more believers than those who are called "Baptists"), and this book will argue in favor of that position. I wanted to make this book as accessible as possible, and as such I do not attempt to answer every possible objection or include references to all (or even much) of the scholarly research that is available.

For a much more comprehensive study on the baptistic position, I recommend that you read *Believer's Baptism: Sign of the New Covenant in Christ*. The book is part of the NAC Studies in Bible and Theology and was edited by Thomas R. Schreiner and Shawn D. Wright.

Section Two
How Should Baptism Be Observed?

3
Whom Should Be Baptized?

In the first section, I argued that baptism was taught as an ordinance by Jesus, the apostles, and the authors of the New Testament. I then showed from Scripture that while baptism is an important symbol, it is not a work that earns the favor of God.

In the following paragraphs, I will seek to demonstrate the Bible's clarity on whom should be baptized. Those who hold to a baptistic view believe the Scriptures teach that only those who make a credible profession of faith should be baptized. A credible profession of faith can be defined as *the claim to trust in Jesus Christ alone for salvation from sin and reconciliation with God, and is accompanied by biblical repentance.* Faith and repentance are two sides of the same coin and are essential to salvation, and therefore essential to baptism – the important symbol of God's saving work in one's life.

This view is in contrast to the paedobaptistic position, which is held and has been held by many genuine believers for centuries. The term paedobaptist (quite a mouthful) places the term *paedo* (meaning "child") before the word baptist. Paedobaptists believe that the children of believers, rather than those who make a credible profession of faith, should be baptized. Since this book is arguing *for* the baptistic position and not *directly against* the paedobaptistic position, the reasons paedobaptists give for holding this view will not be examined or critiqued here. It should be said, again, that genuine believers do hold to a paedobaptistic position, and that many embrace it or continue to embrace it after serious study of Scripture and Christian history.

However, I believe that the paedobaptistic position is unbiblical, and I will make the argument from Jesus' example and teaching, the Scriptural symbolism of baptism, and Luke's historical accounts of baptism.

Jesus' Example and Teaching

In Matthew 3:13-17, we find:

> Then Jesus came from Galilee to the Jordan to John, to be baptized by him. John would have prevented him, saying, "I need to be baptized by you, and do you come to me?" But Jesus answered him, "Let it be so now, for thus it is fitting for us to fulfill all righteousness." Then John consented. And when Jesus was baptized, immediately he went up from the water, and behold, the heavens were opened to him, and he saw the Spirit of God descending like a dove and coming to rest on him; and behold, a voice from heaven said, "This is my beloved Son, with whom I am well pleased."

For many people, Jesus' baptism is a source of great confusion. Why *was* Jesus baptized by John? This is a good question, because even John himself was confused. There are, no doubt, many reasons why Jesus went to be baptized by John, but we'll just consider what is significant to our question. At this time, John wasn't the only guy baptizing. There were many people and groups of people who were baptizing followers. However, John's baptism was unique. He was, as Matthew 3:1-3 declares, the messenger God sent to prepare the way for the Messiah. Jesus went to be baptized by John to affirm John's ministry as the messenger whom God had indeed sent to prepare the way for him.

This explains why Jesus went to John to be baptized. But John didn't understand that, and he did not want to baptize Jesus. So Jesus says, "Let it be so now, for this is fitting for us to fulfill all righteousness," and John baptized him. What we must understand is that Jesus did all things perfectly, not all things pretty well. When Jesus was an infant, he was circumcised on the eighth day according to the Law of Moses and then presented in the temple after the days of purification (Luke 2:21-24). If God desired to establish a pattern of infant baptism, he would have had his own Son baptized as an infant, not as a thirty year old man. His own example makes a strong case for the baptistic view of baptism.

Jesus' teaching also makes a strong case against infant baptism. In Matthew 28:19-20, Jesus commands,

> Go therefore and make disciples of all nations, baptizing them in the name of the Father and of the Son and of the Holy Spirit, teaching them to observe all that I have commanded you. And behold, I am with you always, to the end of the age.

The sequence of Jesus' words is of utmost importance. Jesus commands his followers to make disciples, people that submit to Jesus as Lord and Savior. Then, Jesus says that we are to baptize *them* in the name of the Father, Son, and Holy Spirit. Whom does the Lord command us to baptize? Not the children of disciples, but the disciples themselves. We are to make disciples and baptize *them*. Jesus' example and teaching point strongly to baptizing men and women who have made a credible profession of faith, not infants or children who have made no profession of faith – regardless of whether their parents have.

The Scriptural Symbolism of Baptism

Perhaps the strongest case for a baptistic understanding can be found in Paul's explanation of the symbolism of baptism. He states,

> Do you not know that all of us who have been baptized into Christ Jesus were baptized into his death? We were buried therefore with him by baptism into death, in order that, just as Christ was raised from the dead by the glory of the Father, we too might walk in newness of life (Rom. 6:3-4).

Paul clearly explains that baptism is symbolic of dying with Christ (being "buried" under the water) and then being raised from the dead (being "raised" out of the water). Unless the Bible teaches baptismal regeneration, which it does not, there is no way to make the biblical case that infants should be baptized. According to Romans 6:3-4, baptism is an outward sign of the inward change that has taken place in a believer. No infant has been buried with Christ and raised to walk in newness of life because no infant has repented of sin and believed the Gospel, which is a believer's response to God's work in his or her life.

In his letter to the Colossians, Paul gives a similar explanation. He says,

> In him also you were circumcised with a circumcision made without hands, by putting off the body of the flesh, by the circumcision of Christ, having been buried with him in baptism, in which you were also raised with him through faith in the

powerful working of God, who raised him from the dead (Col. 2:11-12).

Contextually, Paul is most certainly talking about believers, for he refers to those who "were circumcised with a circumcision made without hands." He likens that work to baptism, which represents our burial and resurrection with Christ. And how were we raised with Christ? Paul is clear: "*through faith* in the powerful working of God." Baptism is inseparably connected with faith in Christ in this passage just as it was in Paul's letter to the Romans.

The Scriptural Examples of Baptism

Finally, we will consider three examples from the book of Acts that make a strong case for believers' baptism. These examples highlight Peter's Pentecost sermon, Philip's encounter with the Samaritans, and Philip's encounter with the Ethiopian eunuch.

First, at the outset of Acts 2, Luke records that the day of Pentecost had arrived. In the city of Jerusalem, devout Jews from every nation had gathered to celebrate the occasion. The Holy Spirit falls on the followers of Jesus in the presence of all these Jews, and they began to speak in other languages. In fact, every person present heard the believers speaking "the mighty works of God" in their own languages (2:11). Some accuse the followers of Jesus of being drunk with wine, so Peter takes advantage of the situation to preach the good news about Jesus.

What is critical for our discussion is what Peter exhorts the listeners to do in verse 38: he tells them, "Repent and be baptized." So were all those present baptized? No, they were not. Luke states, "So *those who received his word were baptized*, and there were added that day about three thousand souls" (2:41). The disciples did not baptize everyone there, nor did they baptize the children of those who believed, but only "those who received his word."

Second, in Acts 8, Philip proclaims the Gospel in Samaria. Verses 12-13 note, "But when they believed Philip…they were baptized, both men and women. Even Simon himself believed, and after being baptized he continued with Philip." It is clear in these verses that the Samaritans, including Simon, were baptized after they believed, not simply after they heard Philip's preaching. It is also noteworthy that Luke states, "both men and women" were baptized. One might argue that Luke is simply trying to demonstrate that Christianity is not limited to men in a patriarchal society, but that is unlikely. He has already demonstrated in his first book, the Gospel of Luke (Acts 1:1), that Jesus welcomed women and children (cf. Lk. 8:1-3, 18:15-16). It is more likely that Luke's words demonstrate his understanding that believers, not the children of believers, were to be baptized.

Third and finally, Philip encounters an Ethiopian eunuch and preaches the Gospel to him later in Acts 8. The eunuch asks to be baptized in verse 36. Luke records the interaction between Philip and the eunuch in verse 37 (which is found in some, but not nearly all, reliable manuscripts). Philip answers, "If you believe with all your heart, you may.' And he [the eunuch] replied, 'I believe that Jesus Christ is the Son of God.'"

It is beyond the scope of this book to prove whether or not this verse should be included in the canon of Scripture. What can be said with certainty about this verse is well-stated by H.A. Ironside:

> Scholars generally say it is not recognized as part of reliable Scripture; but inasmuch as it was found in many manuscripts dating back to the early Christian era, it tells us the attitude of the early Church concerning this question.[6]

Ironside draws an appropriate conclusion: the early church believed professing Christians, not infants, should be baptized. The Scriptures and church history both argue in favor of believer's baptism.

Summary and A Look Ahead

From Jesus' example and teaching, the Scriptural symbolism of baptism, and the Scriptural examples of baptism, we can conclude that those who give a credible profession of faith should be baptized, not unbelievers or the children of believers.

While many Christians agree that only professing believers should be baptized, there is disagreement over whether or not the *mode* of baptism is important (i.e. whether we sprinkle, dip, or immerse believers in water). In chapter four, we will consider the Scriptural teaching on how believers should be baptized.

---

[6] Ironside, H.A. *Lectures on Acts*. New Jersey: Loizeaux Brothers, 1982, 197.

4

How Should We Baptize?

In chapter three, we learned from Scripture that those who give a credible profession of faith should be baptized – not unbelievers or the children of believers. In this chapter, we will consider the mode of baptism. Some believers are persuaded that the mode of baptism is important (typically those who hold to a baptistic position, but not always), while other believers do not think the mode of baptism matters. As long as we are baptizing those who make a credible profession of faith, they say, why does it matter whether we sprinkle, dip, or submerge people? I will argue that the mode of baptism *is* important because of what is represented in baptism.

The Meaning of the Word Baptize

When the word "baptize" appears in your English Bible, you are reading a transliteration of the Greek word *baptizo*. Regrettably, this word has been transliterated rather than translated from the Greek. Transliteration is the practice of taking a word in one language and devising a phonetical (sound) equivalent in another language. You can easily see how we got "baptize" from *baptizo* since the two words sound nearly identical. However, if this word had been translated (where the meaning, not the sound, of the word was rendered) into English rather than transliterated, we would have something like "immerse" or "submerge," not "baptize," for that is what *baptizo* actually means. This word was used in the garment-dying industry to describe the process of changing the color of fabric: it was "baptized" in a bucket of dye. If someone wanted to change the color of a garment, he or she would not sprinkle it or dip it into the bucket, but would "baptize" it, completely immersing it under the dye.

Obviously, transliterating this Greek word has left most English readers confused on the mode of baptism. The meaning of the word baptize, however, explains exactly how baptism should be performed – by immersion. Consider B.H. Carroll's statement on this discussion: "Baptism is one definite thing – immersion – and not permissibly one of three things: sprinkling, pouring, or immersion."[7]

Scriptural Evidence for the Mode of Baptism

Immersion is seen to be the only mode of baptism in the Gospels and the Book of Acts through the references to John's baptism and the historical account of Philip and the Ethiopian eunuch.

First, we will consider Luke's references to the baptism of John in the Book of Acts. Luke refers to John's baptism explicitly seven times in the Book of Acts, and may refer to it in several other instances.[8] According to these references, John baptized with water. All Christians are agreed on the fact that baptism should be done with water, but how the water should be applied sparks great disagreement.

The Gospel writers provide several convincing pieces of evidence concerning the proper mode of baptism. Writing about John the Baptist,

---

[7] Carroll, B.H. Baptists and Their Doctrines, ed. Timothy and Denise George (Nashville: Broadman and Holman, 1999), 135.

[8] 1:5, 1:22, 10:37, 11:16, 13:24, 18:25, 19:3, 19:4, 19:5

Luke states, "And he went into all the region *around the Jordan*, proclaiming a baptism of repentance for the forgiveness of sins" (Luke 3:3). It is significant that Luke notes John conducted his ministry to the area around major sources of water like the Jordan River. If he were merely sprinkling or pouring water on those who wished to publicly proclaim their repentance, he could have traveled far and wide with a small container of water. However, John stayed close to the Jordan and other large sources of water because he was immersing repentant men and women, not sprinkling or pouring water on them. Luke, who wrote this Gospel, is the same author who wrote the Book of Acts, and it is unlikely Luke's understanding of the proper mode of baptism changed between the two writings.

The Apostle John agrees with this understanding as well. In 3:23, he writes, "John also was baptizing at Aenon near Salim, *because water was plentiful there*, and people were coming to him to be baptized." Again, to sprinkle or pour, one does not need plentiful water. Further, Mark and Matthew note that John's baptism was taking place "*in the river Jordan*" and that Jesus "*came up out of* the water" after his baptism.[9] It is likely that Luke was aware of Matthew and Mark's accounts and does not disagree with their presentation of baptism in his own Gospel or the Book of Acts.

Second, Philip's encounter with the Ethiopian eunuch demonstrates Luke's understanding of baptism very clearly. After Philip

---

[9] Thomas R. Schreiner and Shawn D. Wright, eds., NAC Studies in Bible & Theology, *Believer's Baptism: Sign of the New Covenant in Christ* (Nashville: Broadman and Holman, 2006), 60.

preaches the Gospel to the eunuch, the Ethiopian exclaims, "See, *here* is water! What prevents me from being baptized?" (Acts 8:36). If Philip was going to sprinkle or pour water on the eunuch, they would not have needed to stop. Surely a man traveling many miles by chariot in the desert would have brought drinking water simply to survive the long journey (Acts 8:26-28). Moreover, verses 38-39 say, "…and they both *went down* into the water, Philip and the eunuch, and he baptized him. And *when they came up out of the water*…". The two men went down into the water, Philip baptized him, and then they came up out of the water. Going all the way into the water would have been unnecessary if only a sprinkle or small amount for pouring was sufficient.

Summary and A Look Ahead

Apart from the weight of the actual definition of the Greek word *baptizo*, it is obvious in the four Gospels and the Book of Acts that baptism is presented as having one acceptable mode – immersion. John immersed repentant men and women, as Philip clearly did with the Ethiopian eunuch. We can conclude that Bible presents baptism as having one acceptable mode – immersion in water.

Now that we have considered whom should be baptized and how one should be baptized, we will conclude part two by answering the question, "When should a believer be baptized?"

5

When Should We Baptize?

At the outset of this book, baptism was shown to be an ordinance, or command, of Jesus to every Christian. If baptism is a command of Christ to every believer, then it is to be obeyed without delay, not postponed until a more convenient time. In the first few centuries of the church, it was the practice of some professing believers, such as Emperor Constantine, to wait to be baptized until the last possible moment of their lives. This was due in part to the unbiblical idea that sins committed after baptism would not be forgiven by God.

The practice of the early church, as recorded in Acts, was to administer baptism as soon as possible after one made a profession of faith in Jesus.[10] In the follow paragraphs, Peter, Philip, and Paul's practices will be recounted and explained.

Peter's Practice

Peter's practice was to preach that believers should be baptized as soon as possible after conversion. In Acts 2:38, Peter commands the believers to "repent and be baptized," and three thousand people responded to his exhortation that day (2:41). Luke does not give any indication that delaying baptism was an option; he simply presents it in Peter's sermon as an ordinance that should be observed by professing

---

[10] Green, Michael. *Thirty Years that Changed the World: The Book of Acts for Today* (Grand Rapids: Eerdmans, 2002), 166).

believers without delay. Peter carried this same understanding with him when he went to preach to Cornelius and his household. When he saw the evidence of the Holy Spirit in the words and actions of these Gentiles, Peter exclaimed, "Can anyone withhold water for baptizing these people, who have received the Holy Spirit just as we have?" (10:47). Peter's implication is that baptism should not be delayed by any person or for any reason; it is an ordinance that is to be observed as soon as possible after conversion.[11]

Philip's Practice

Philip's words and actions support Peter's understanding and practice as well. The Ethiopian eunuch, either because Philip explained his need to be baptized or because he understood its symbolism and significance from the Old Testament and culture, asked Philip to be baptized as soon as they came to abundant water.

In his encounter with the Samaritans, Philip preached the Gospel to them, and *after* they believed, they were baptized (Acts 8:12-13.). Even Simon the magician, whose profession of faith is questioned by many scholars, was baptized along with the others. Philip does not tell them to wait, but baptizes them once they professed faith in Christ – even though the Holy Spirit had not yet fallen on them! Luke tells his readers that the church in Jerusalem sent Peter and John to pray that these believers would receive the Holy Spirit, but Philip does not wait for them to arrive. If baptism was not to be practiced as soon as possible after conversion,

---

[11] Criswell, W.A. *Acts: An Exposition*, vol. I. Grand Rapids: Zondervan, 1978, 97.

then surely Philip would have waited until Peter and John (who were Apostles) arrived to pray for them.

Paul's Practice

Finally, Paul understood that baptism should be practiced as soon as possible after conversion. After Ananias preached to Paul on Straight Street and the scales fell from his eyes, Paul regained his sight. Then Luke records, "he rose and was baptized" (9:18). Significantly, Paul does not eat first, though he had taken no food for three days. He is immediately baptized after he believes in Jesus. Additionally, when Paul preaches to the Philippian jailer in Acts 16, Luke explains that he was baptized "at once" after believing the message (v. 33). This is significant not just because he was baptized immediately after believing the Gospel, but also because this incident occurred in the middle of the night (v. 25). Last, when Paul explained to the disciples of John the Baptist in Ephesus that they needed to be baptized in the name of the Lord Jesus, the twelve men responded "on hearing this" (19:5). They did not needlessly delay baptism.

Summary

Peter, Philip, and Paul clearly believed that baptism should be observed as soon as possible after conversion. I have been using the term "as soon as possible" rather than a word like "immediately" because I do not intend to communicate that a person is in sin if he or she is not baptized immediately after conversion. This is for several reasons:

1) Baptism is not a work that saves or contributes to salvation, as discussed in chapters one and two. The thief on the cross (Luke 23:39-43) was not baptized at all, and Jesus promised that he would be with Him in Paradise.

2) While conversion is an act of God that happens at a particular point in time, believers are not always certain when exactly they were converted. The most common example is children growing up in Christian homes. A boy or girl may genuinely repent and trust in Christ at an early age, but not be able to fully articulate their faith until later in life. They should be baptized when they and their parents believe their profession of faith credible.

3) Baptizing people indiscriminately may lead to giving false assurance to men and women who are not genuinely converted. There is no way to ensure that only genuinely converted people are baptized, since only God knows those who are His. However, Christian leaders should make appropriate inquiry into a person's profession of faith prior to baptizing them. Leaders could speak with someone who has professed faith in Christ immediately or at some later point. When the inquiry is made is not what is most important; *that* an inquiry is made is. Neglecting to speak with someone who has made a profession of faith to ensure they understand the Gospel is not a good practice.

4) There are cases when people are not able to be baptized immediately (such as illness, injury, etc.) or when baptizing

them immediately would not be wise. Say, for example, a college student professes faith in Christ and wants to be baptized. It would be very disrespectful to baptize them if his or her parents were believers, had been praying for their child for years, and wanted to be present at his or her baptism.

Of course, there are many other factors that must be considered as well. What I intend to communicate is that the Scriptures are clear that believers should not *needlessly* postpone baptism. It is an ordinance of Christ, and the clear teaching and example of the New Testament is that believers should be baptized as soon as possible after conversion.

Final Thoughts

I'm a pastor in a local church. I'm not a famous author, and I don't have any formal training as a writer outside my basic high school and undergraduate writing courses. Writing this book has been a long, difficult process, but I hope that it has served you well.

I am convinced that while baptism is not crucial to the Christian life, it is important because it is commanded by the Lord Jesus. I believe a baptistic understanding of baptism, as articulated in this book, is most faithful to Biblical teaching and example. I disagree with theologians like Wayne Grudem who believe that baptistic churches should open their membership to those who hold a paedobaptistic position.[12] However, I do believe that local churches with similar theology but different

---

[12] Grudem, *Systematic Theology*, 982-3.

understandings of baptism can and should work together for the advancement of the Gospel. My own church, New Life, models this commitment through our membership in the Acts 29 Network (www.acts29network.org), our partnership with ministries like 9 Marks (www.9marks.org), and our friendship with local churches like Westminster PCA (www.wpc-bryan.org).

Thank you for taking time to read this book. In the appendix, you will find answers to the most common questions I receive about baptism. I hope that you will find it practical and helpful.

Appendix
Answers to Specific Questions about Baptism

As a pastor in a local church, I get lots of questions that don't have easy answers. In this section, I will answer the most common questions I receive about baptism. I hope that you find this section is helpful for you or for others you know who are asking these same questions.

I've been a Christian for many years now but was never baptized. Do I really need to be baptized?

I start with this question because this is the very question I asked my pastor when I had been a Christian for about two years. I had been baptized in a Roman Catholic Church as an infant and became a believer at the age of 19 while I was a freshman at Texas A&M. By the time I came to understand that the Bible taught believers should be baptized by immersion in water after conversion, I was a junior in college. Even though I had not been baptized, I reasoned that the point of baptism was to make a public profession of faith, and by my junior year of college everyone in my life knew that I was a believer.

Sitting in a ministry preparation course with my pastor and some of my peers, my reasoning was challenged. My pastor and my peers pointed me to Matthew 28:18-20, where Jesus commands believers to be baptized in the name of the Father, Son, and Holy Spirit. I had not been baptized as a believer; I had been sprinkled as an unbelieving infant.

Further, I was implicitly stating that obedience to the Scriptures is not necessary if you have delayed your obedience long enough.

I realized that I needed to be baptized because Jesus commanded every believer to be baptized by immersion in water after conversion. His commands are not optional, and I had made obedience optional by my actions. I repented of my disobedience and was baptized in Rudder Fountain (on the campus of Texas A&M University) in November 2002 along with several others from my church.

If you have been a believer for many years and have never been baptized by immersion in water after your conversion, you need to repent and obey Jesus' words as well. It may not seem like a big deal to you or someone you know, but Jesus does not command frivolous activities. Baptism is a symbolic display of God's regenerative work, and it is important both for the believer and those who witness the baptism.

I was sprinkled/poured as an infant. Do I need to be "rebaptized?"

If you were sprinkled or poured as an infant, it's not accurate to say that you were "baptized." If you were sprinkled or poured as an infant, you were never baptized for three reasons:

> **1) Sprinkling and pouring are misapplications of the Greek word for "baptize."** As we discussed in chapter four, the Greek word *baptizo* means "to submerge or immerse." There is no way to conclude that a proper application of that word is to sprinkle or pour water on someone. If you were sprinkled with water or

had water poured over you, you were not immersed, and therefore you were not "baptized."

2) Sprinkling and pouring do violence to the meaning of baptism. According to Romans 6 and Colossians 2, baptism is a picture of being dead in sin and raised to walk in new life. Sprinkling or pouring water might represent washing, but they most certainly do not represent being dead and then raised to life again.

3) Baptism is to be performed on those who have made a credible profession of faith. Because baptism is symbolic of what God has done to a believer (and not symbolic of what one day might happen to a particular person), sprinkling or pouring water on infants performs an act that should be reserved for believers.

If you were sprinkled or poured as an infant (or, for that matter, if you were sprinkled or poured at any time), you need to be baptized by immersion in water in obedience to the Scriptures.

"I was baptized by immersion in a church that teaches a salvific view of baptism. Do I need to be baptized again?"

Without a doubt, this is one of the hardest questions to answer definitively. The Church of Christ baptizes by immersion (the proper mode), but teaches that baptism is essential to salvation. We have already seen in chapter two that baptism is not essential to salvation, since Jesus promised the unbaptized thief on the cross that he would be with him in

Paradise and since Paul makes a clear distinction between baptism and the Gospel in 1 Corinthians 1. There is no question that baptismal regeneration is a heretical teaching.

What needs to be determined is what you believed when you were baptized. Did you believe that baptism was a work you performed to earn salvation? If so, you most certainly need to be baptized again. You were trusting in works to save you and not relying on Christ's finished work alone, which Paul calls "another Gospel." You were not baptized as a believer, and therefore were not truly baptized.

However, if you were baptized in a heretical church out of obedience to Christ, not for salvation, then I do not believe you need to be baptized again. It seems, in that case, that you believed the true Gospel in a heretical church, which has happened throughout Christian history. Many believers were saved in the Roman Catholic Church during the reformation period, yet the Roman Catholic Church did not and does not adhere to the true Gospel. The answer to this question hinges on what you believed about Christ and the nature of baptism when you were baptized.

"I was baptized by immersion, but I wasn't a believer at the time. Do I need to be baptized again?"

The Scriptures are clear that baptism is to be performed on believers. Baptism is not an initiation rite that is performed on those who want entrance into a club or organization. It is symbolic of God's regenerating work that has already taken place in the life of a believer. If you were baptized before you repented and believed the Gospel, you weren't baptized – you took a really quick bath in front of a church with no soap and your clothes on. You need to be baptized biblically, which means you need to be obedient to Christ who has commanded believers to be baptized.

"I'm not sure if I was converted when I was baptized. What should I do?"

Because our church is in Texas (the so-called "buckle" of the Bible belt), many people were baptized at a young age. Some were baptized after a genuine conversion, while others were baptized for different reasons, including:

1) As an emotional response to a moving evangelistic rally or sermon.

2) To please their parents.

3) To fulfill cultural expectations.

4) To get a reward of some kind.[13]

If it were easy to discern that one had been baptized for one of the reasons above, and not because of genuine repentance and faith in Jesus, people wouldn't have a hard time determining if they should be baptized. Obviously, getting baptized for one of the reasons above is getting baptized with the wrong motivation. Unfortunately, for some

---

[13] Tom Ascol, "Of Fire Engine Baptistries And Blasphemy," *Founders Ministries*, May 7, 2006, http://www.founders.org/blog/2006/05/of-fire-engine-baptistries-and.html. (accessed October 1, 2009).

people it just isn't very clear in their minds why they were baptized if they were baptized at a young age, and that may be true for you as well.

My advice to people struggling to determine whether or not they were truly converted when they were baptized is not easy, but it is simple: you need to spend time in serious reflection on your life before and after you were baptized, then prayerfully evaluate your life based on the Word of God. Paul states in 2 Corinthians 7:9-11:

> As it is, I rejoice, not because you were grieved, but because you were grieved into repenting. For you felt a godly grief, so that you suffered no loss through us. For godly grief produces a repentance that leads to salvation without regret, whereas worldly grief produces death. For see what earnestness this godly grief has produced in you, but also what eagerness to clear yourselves, what indignation, what fear, what longing, what zeal, what punishment! At every point you have proved yourselves innocent in the matter.

Paul is clear that there are two kinds of grief brought on by the knowledge of sin: a godly grief that produces a repentance that leads to salvation without regret, and a worldly grief that produces death. True repentance (godly grief) means that you not only feel sorrow for your sin, but you confess your sin to God and others and by his grace live differently afterward. False repentance (worldly grief) means that you feel bad about your sin, but after a little time passes or your conscience tells you that you really aren't that bad, you revert back to the same old sins. If you were truly repentant and genuinely converted when you were baptized, you do not need to be baptized. If, on the other hand, you had mere worldly grief, you were *not* converted and you do need to be baptized.

It is important to restate here that this is no easy question to answer, and you must keep in mind that what is most important is that you have truly repented and believed in Christ *today*. Baptism is an ordinance of Christ, so it is important, but it is not an issue of salvation, so it is not of ultimate importance. Whatever you decide about the state of your soul at your baptism, you need to be fully convinced in your own mind and put the issue to rest. The worst thing you can do is continually doubt whether or not you were truly converted when you were baptized the rest of your life.

"I am still dependent on my parents and they do not want me to be baptized because...

1) ...they say that I was baptized as an infant and it would dishonor them if I was baptized again."

America is a very religious nation. While there are likely relatively few genuine believers in our nation, many here profess to believe and adhere outwardly to some kind of religious system. While their faith does not have any noticeable impact on their day-to-day lives, many parents are offended when their children do not adopt the same faith system and practices to which they adhere.

In my experience, children who were sprinkled or poured as infants who approach their parents and ask to be baptized are usually met with at least some resistance. Most parents want to know why their children want to be baptized, then state that they have already been baptized, referring to their infant sprinkling or pouring rite. If the issue is pressed further, some parents are willing to let their children be baptized, while others refuse.

If your parents have refused to allow you to be baptized, my advice is that you take time to pray for your own motivation, attitude, and means of approach. Going to your parents and asking to be baptized in an attempt to prove them wrong, "get back at them," or to show them you're really spiritual are all wrong motivations. It's very important to remember your place: you are their child, and as such, you are bound by Scripture to honor them always (Ex. 20:12, Matt. 15:1-9). During and after your prayers, you need to study the Scriptures to show them why you believe it to be important that you are baptized. You can also use chapters 2-5 of this book to help you.

After praying for them and for yourself, go to them in a spirit of humility. Speaking gently and respectfully to them, show them from the Scriptures why baptism is important to you. I have seen very few cases where a child has approached his or her parents in a spirit of humility and with Scriptural reasons in hand and been denied permission to be baptized. However, it does happen on occasion, and if your parents will not allow you to be baptized, then you have to decide whether or not you are willing to be "cut off" financially and relationally from your parents to be obedient to Christ. This decision should not be made quickly or in isolation, but only after spending considerable time searching the Scriptures, praying, and receiving counsel from elders in your church.

2) ...they say that they do not want me becoming some kind of radical Christian."

Most parents assume that when their child comes home with a fresh wardrobe of Christian t-shirts, a new cross necklace, and a big ole' study Bible that this is just a phase and will soon pass. They reason that they have watched you get excited about things for a few months your entire life, and that you will be back to your old self soon enough, and the Christian stuff you accumulated will earn a spot next to your high school accolades at the top of your closet.

When they realize that this "phase" is the real deal, some parents will be pleased to see the changes that God has brought to your life. Other parents will react negatively, believing that your conversion is an indictment on the way they raised you or their own beliefs. If you receive this latter reaction, you need to understand that we live in a society that tolerates moderation in everything and extremes in nothing – except sin. Further, the only people your parents may have exposure to who are as passionate about their faith as you are may be the Muslim extremists they see on the nightly news. When you put these two realities together you have a recipe for a concerned, if not downright antagonistic, parent.

You need to put your parents' concerns to rest by praying for them regularly, speaking to them about your faith and your desire to be baptized as God gives opportunity, and allow your changed life to do most of the talking. Your parents have known you your entire life, and the only people that change overnight have been changed by God. Let them observe your grateful spirit, your respectful tone, your desire to love and serve them, and then approach them again about being baptized. Once they see that Christ has changed you for good and not for evil, they will probably be much more open to you being baptized.

I'm a parent, and my young child has professed faith in Christ. Should I seek to have him/her baptized or wait until he/she is older?

This is a very tough question. On the one hand, I believe the Bible teaches that baptism should be performed as soon as possible after conversion. On the other hand, I believe that only those who make a credible profession of faith should be baptized, and that is difficult to determine when dealing with young children.

Many good churches, like Capitol Hill Baptist Church in Washington, D.C. have thoughtfully articulated a biblical and wise position on this issue.[14] I encourage you to read their entire statement (entitled "The Baptism of Children at CHBC (2004)"), but here is a brief excerpt that will help you understand their position:

> We believe that the normal age of baptism should be when the credibility of one's conversion becomes naturally evident to the church community. This would normally be when the child has

---

[14] *Capitol Hill Baptist Church*, 2004, "Baptism Of Children," http://www.capitolhillbaptist.org/we-equip/children/baptism-of-children// (accessed October 1, 2009).

matured, and is beginning to live more self-consciously as an individual, making their own choices, having left the God-given, intended child-like dependence on their parents for the God-given, intended mature wisdom which marks one who has felt the tug of the world, the flesh and the devil, but has decided, despite these allurements, to follow Christ. While it is difficult to set a certain number of years which are required for baptism, it is appropriate to consider the candidate's maturity. The kind of maturity that we feel it is wise to expect is the maturity which would allow that son or daughter to deal directly with the church as a whole, and not, fundamentally, to be under their parents' authority. As they assume adult responsibilities (sometime in late high school with driving, employment, non-Christian friends, voting, legality of marriage), then part of this, we would think, would be to declare publicly their allegiance to Christ by baptism.

Children who make a profession of faith should be baptized when they, their parents, and their leaders in the church believe their profession is credible. It would be unhelpful to set a particular age for baptism, as that would encourage some to be baptized before they were genuinely converted and others to needlessly delay their baptism. On this issue, carefully searching the Scriptures, praying, and seeking wisdom from leaders in the church is the best way to make a decision on the appropriate time to baptize your young child who has professed faith in Christ.

Made in United States
Orlando, FL
26 August 2024